JUL 17 1999

LOS GATOS PUBLIC LIBRARY
Telephone: 408-354-6891

A fine shall be charged each day an item is kept overtime. No item will be issued to persons in arrears for fines.

Loss of, or damage to an item other than regular wear and tear, must be paid by the person to whom the book is charged.

Attention is called to the rule that items borrowed from the library must not be loaned.

For violation of these rules, the privileges of the library may be withdrawn from any person at any time.

GAYLORD F

ALL
ABOARD
READING™

Level 2
Grades 1-3

WAGON TRAIN

By Sydelle Kramer
Illustrated by Deborah Kogan Ray

Grosset & Dunlap • New York

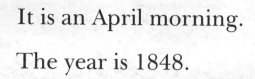

It is an April morning.

The year is 1848.

A long, long line of wagons
rumbles down the trail.
Hundreds of people are on board.

They are pioneers.

(You say it like this: pie-uh-NEERS.)

They're leaving their old homes behind

to start a new life.

Every one of them is excited.

They're moving west to California!

The pioneers have heard great things

about California.

It is green and beautiful.

The sun shines all year long.

People can get land there for free.

They might even get rich!

But the trip is long and hard.

California is two thousand miles away.

It takes six months to reach it.

There's no road—just a dirt trail.

The wagons have cloth covers
to keep out wind, rain, and sun.
The pioneers call them covered wagons.
From far away,
they look like sailboats against the sky.

The wagon train moves slowly—
just ten or fifteen miles a day.
The trail is full of holes and bumps.
The wagons sway and buck.
Children hold on tight to the sides.

The wagons are heavy.

Oxen pull them.

Oxen walk slowly,

but they're stronger than horses.

Why do the wagons weigh so much?

They're jammed with everything

the pioneers need for their new life.

There are tables, chairs, and beds,

chests, washtubs, and even clocks.

Barrels and sacks are stuffed

with sugar, flour, and beans.

It's so crowded inside,

there's hardly room for people.

The wagon train comes to a stop.

Ahead is a deep river.

The water crashes and swirls!

There's no bridge or ferry.

How will the pioneers get across?

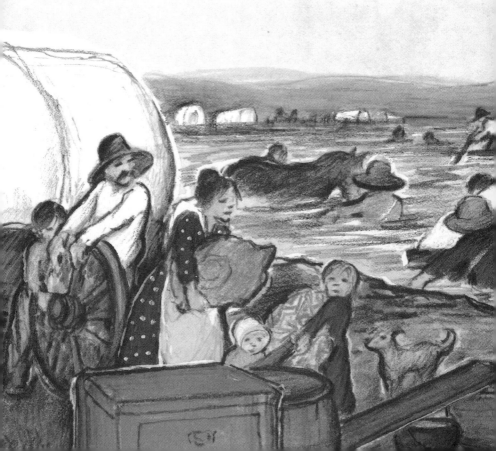

They unpack the wagons.

They take some of them apart.

Everything is floated over on rafts.

It will take hours to get to the other side—

and hours to put the wagons back together.

Crossing the river is dangerous.

Not everyone can swim.

One raft suddenly slams into a rock,

and a young man falls off.

The water sweeps him away.

He's dragged under and drowned.

But the wagons have to keep rolling.
The pioneers must reach California
before winter.
Once snow starts to fall,
wagons can get stuck on the trail.

It's hard to think of winter now.

The sun is boiling hot.

There are bugs everywhere.

The pioneers are crossing

the Great Plains.

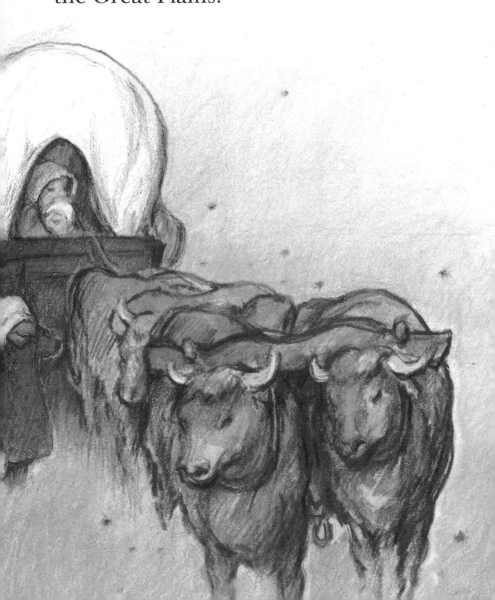

For weeks and weeks,

the pioneers never see a hill or a tree.

All they see is miles of grass—

and millions of buffalo.

It takes six days to pass some herds.

Terrible storms slow the pioneers down.
One day, hailstones as big as eggs
pound their heads.

The very next night,
lightning burns up a wagon.

It rains so hard,

the ground is like

a muddy stream.

One morning strangers appear.

Indians!

The pioneers grab their guns.

They're afraid.

They have heard that Indians attack

wagon trains.

These Indians don't want to fight.

They have come to trade.

They trade deer meat and

shoes called moccasins

(you say it like this: MOCK-a-sins)

for sugar and cloth.

The chief lights a peace pipe
and smokes it with the pioneers.

Every night the wagons make a circle.

The pioneers put up tents

and gather in the animals.

That way, everyone is safer.

The pioneers wake before sunrise.

The wagons get back on the trail.

Sundays are different.

Sunday is a day of rest.

Holidays are different, too

On the Fourth of July, there are horse race

and shooting contests.

The pioneers play music, sing,
and dance till their feet are sore.

The wagons leave the plains behind.

They come to huge mountains

called the Rockies.

The Rockies are easy to cross—

there's a pass right through them.

But on the other side,

the pioneers aren't sure where to go.

They know whole wagon trains

sometimes get lost here.

Are they still on the right trail?

Yes!

Other wagon trains have been this way.

How do they know?

They see rocks with writing

and sticks with notes

poking out from them.

That's how pioneers leave news behind.

Chests and chairs

are scattered on the ground.

Pioneers have tossed them out

to make their wagons lighter.

There's even a piano standing in the dust.

The pioneers head into the desert.

It's 110 degrees by noon.

The sun burns their skin.

The heat cracks their lips.

Dust covers them like a blanket

and sticks in their throats.

Worst of all,

they're almost out of water!

There are just a few barrels left.

Can they find a water hole soon?

Two days go by.

Then they see

something sparkling up ahead!

It's a desert spring.

Pioneers and animals rush to it

and gulp the fresh water down.

At the end of the desert,

more mountains stand in the way.

There's no pass through them.

But once the pioneers get across,

they'll be in California.

The wagons start climbing.

It gets colder and colder.

Everyone tries to hurry,

but the trail is very steep.

The pioneers must help the oxen

up the mountains.

It's even harder going down!

The wagons don't have any brakes.

If they start to roll fast,

there's no way to stop.

So the pioneers lower

the wagons with ropes.

The pioneers have made it!

They are in California at last.

The land is green and beautiful.

The sun is shining.

Now their new life can begin.

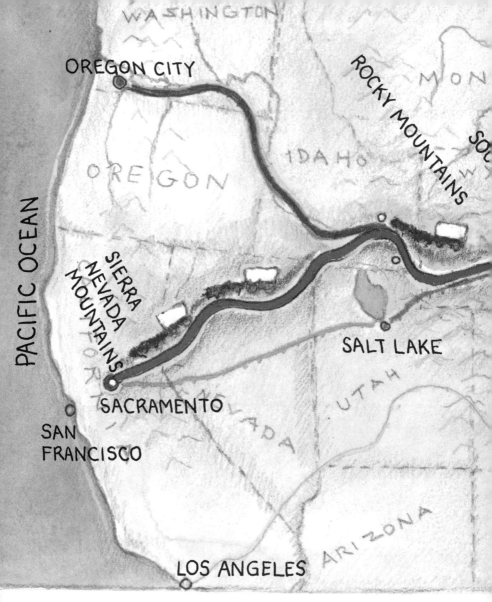

Wagon trains help America grow

from coast to coast.

From 1840 to 1870,

250,000 pioneers move west on wagons.

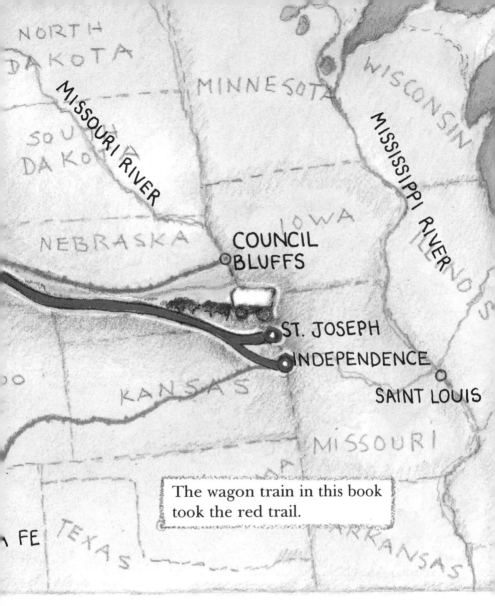

The wagon train in this book took the red trail.

They travel on different trails.

No wagon train is the same size.

Some are as small as four families.

Others are gigantic—five miles long!

When railroads cross the country,

the wagons stop rolling.

But the tracks of their wheels

are still in the ground.

People come from everywhere to see them

and to remember the pioneers.